DIARY OF A RABBIT

DIARY OF A RABBIT

by LILO HESS

Charles Scribner's Sons   New York

Library of Congress Cataloging in Publication Data
Hess, Lilo.   Diary of a rabbit.
Summary: Follows the day-to-day activities of
a rabbit from birth to motherhood.
1. Rabbits—Juvenile literature. [1. Rabbits]
I. Title.
SF453.2.H49   636'.9322   81-9317
ISBN 0-684-17413-8   AACR2

1 3 5 7 9 11 13 15 17 19 Q/C 20 18 16 14 12 10 8 6 4 2

Printed in the United States of America

April 30 Much later in this story the tiny rabbit that had just been born was named Daisy. At this moment she was nameless, wet, and struggling to take a first breath on her own. She weighed two ounces. She was the third rabbit to emerge from her mother's womb in the dark, early morning of the last day in April. Two brothers, born just minutes earlier, were almost dry and pushing to get at their mother's nipples to drink the very rich rabbit's milk. (Rabbit's milk has 1,000 calories per pound; fresh cow's milk has about 350 calories per pound.)

5

Daisy was probably not aware of what went on around her, except perhaps for her mother's warm tongue cleaning and drying her. Then she, too, searched for a nipple and suckled heartily while other brothers and sisters were still being born and cleaned by the mother. In all, seven fawns (baby rabbits) arrived in less than half an hour.

The babies could not see or hear and had no fur. But their skin already showed their future markings and pigment. The pink areas would grow white fur and the darker patterns would be brown or salt-and-pepper; the black areas would be black or bluish-black. Three of the babies would look like their mother, who was of a color called agouti, a dark brown color mixed with lighter shades; four would be white with black patches like their father.

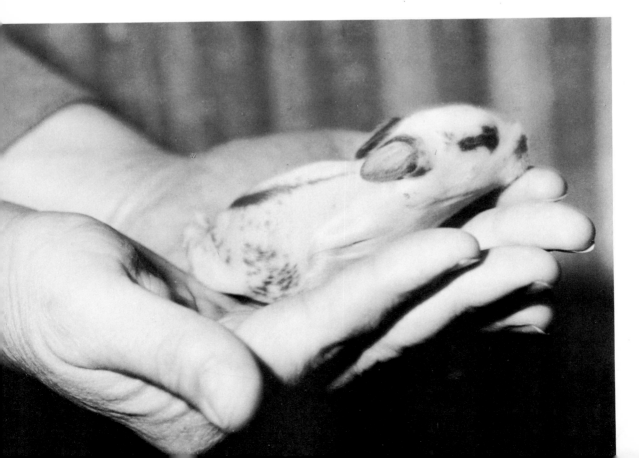

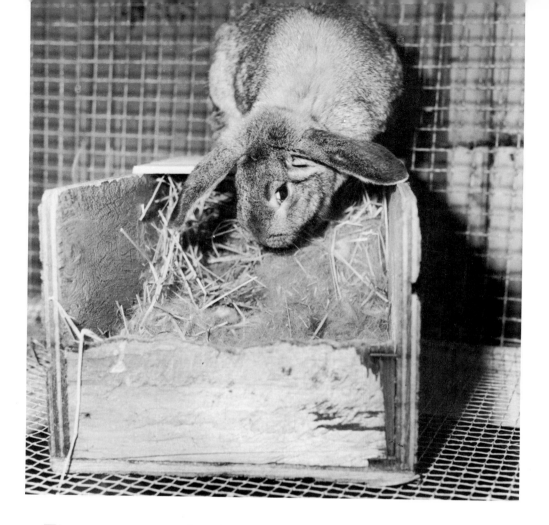

The nest was made of straw, which the rabbit breeder had placed in the narrow, wooden nesting box, and soft, fluffy wisps of fur that the doe (the female rabbit) had plucked from her own chest and abdomen to make a soft, warm lining and cover for her babies.

After all the babies had finished their first meal, they slept. The doe covered them with the fur and jumped on top of the nestbox to guard them. Every hour or so she went back into the nestbox to let the babies nurse.

May 3 On the fourth day the growth of the babies was noticeable. Their fur had started to grow. Their ears were still folded back against the skull, but had become longer. When the breeder picked them up, they wriggled and squirmed vigorously and tried to escape. When they were put back into the nest, they washed their faces with tiny forepaws and cleaned their bodies as if to rid themselves of the human smell. But most of the time the babies slept quietly, huddled together, and only became active at nursing time.

May 10 On the eleventh day most of the babies had their eyes open and hopped and played and sometimes jumped right out of the nest. Each time the mother pushed them back in. They also showed some interest in their mother's food. None of them made any sounds.

8

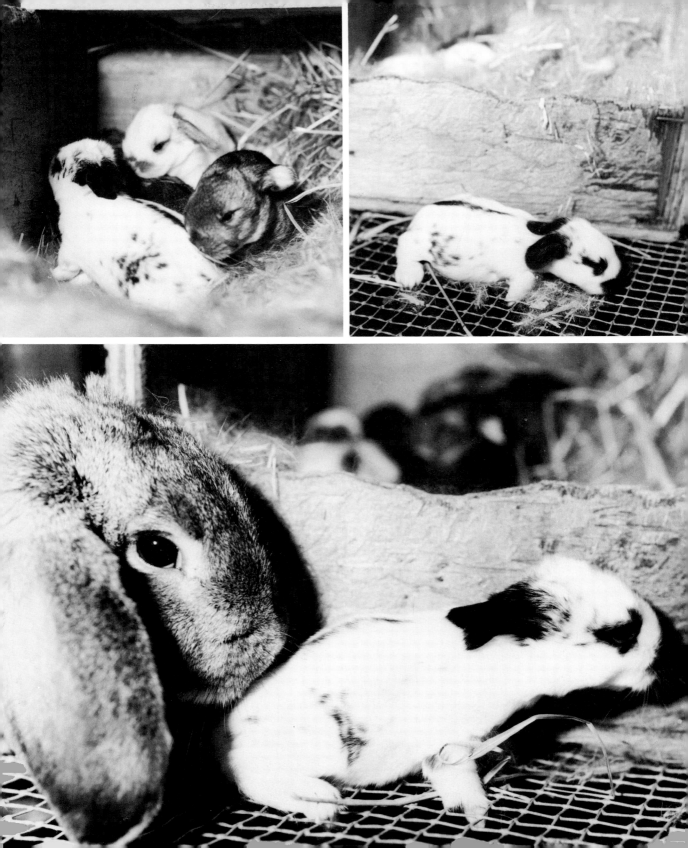

May 19 Daisy and her brothers and sisters had all their fur now. They could hear extremely well and were startled at any unusual noise. Their long, slender ears stood erect, but soon they would fold downward like their mother's, a characteristic of this breed called Mini Lops.

June 11 When the baby rabbits were six weeks old and weaned, the breeder removed them from their mother's pen and placed them in a hutch (a rabbit pen) of their own. The seven little bunnies jumped and played a lot. Like adult rabbits, they ate pellets and nibbled hay and a few leafy greens the breeder provided as a treat. They drank a lot of water. When they were tired, they slept, huddled together. In another few weeks the breeder would have to place each rabbit in a separate pen, because adult rabbits often fight.

June 18 The wind had been howling all night and the noise of falling and cracking branches kept the rabbits awake and uneasy. The young ones sat motionless in a corner of the hutch. Rain came down like a waterfall, and the strong wind blew it in all directions. Many of the rabbits got drenched despite the roof that sheltered all the hutches. Suddenly, a strong gust of wind lifted the young rabbits' cage off its shelf. The little ones were thrown with force against the door, which opened, spilling all of them out just a split second before the hutch hit the ground.

Some babies were flung several feet away, propelled by the force of the wind.

Daisy fell into a thorn bush and her feet, back, and legs were bleeding from scratches. In panic she scurried away across the lawn and across a field until she was exhausted and took shelter under a bush. After she had stopped trembling, she used her front paws to wipe her face and to comb her wet fur with her nails. With her teeth she picked off bits of leaves and twigs that clung to her, and she tried to lick the blood away from her cuts. It was dry under the bush and soon the tired and frightened little rabbit slept.

June 19 The morning after the storm the air was still and cool. Everything looked freshly washed. Daisy emerged cautiously and looked around. The fragrance of wild flowers and clover hung in the air. Small animals and insects were busily gathering food to take to their homes, or they were feeding on

the spot. Some wild cottontail rabbits were playfully jumping over one another or running and chasing each other. Others were munching fresh greens. Daisy wanted to join them and hopped near them, but the wild rabbits ruffled their noses when they got Daisy's scent, turned and hopped away. They wanted no part of her. Daisy followed them at a distance, stopping often to nibble some greens.

Daisy was easily startled. Any unfamiliar sound or object made her dash for shelter or freeze. A buzzing dragonfly, a noisy blue jay, and even a little white-footed mouse who scurried by carrying some dried grass for her nest, made the little rabbit tremble.

June 21   Daisy moved farther and farther away from her old rabbitry. The breeder had retrieved all of Daisy's brothers and sisters and had installed them in new, secure hutches, but he could not find Daisy, and soon stopped looking for her. Like the wild rabbits, Daisy slept under bushes or in the tall grass during the day, and came out to feed at dusk and early dawn.

June 23   Early this June morning Daisy emerged from her shelter, groomed herself, and then hopped about looking for something to eat. She noticed some sweet-smelling plants and hopped over to sample them. It was a bed of gaily colored petunias. The rabbit nibbled on a number of buds, and playfully jumped about, breaking many flowers and pulling some out of the soil with her teeth. After she tired of this game, she hopped on till she came to a wire fence surrounding a vegetable garden. She could smell tantalizing odors from carrots, lettuce, and peas growing in the garden and tried to push through the fence. When this did not work she tried to dig her way into the enclosure, but the ground was too rocky. Suddenly, she stumbled into a depression in the ground and immediately saw the hole in the wire. She squeezed through and at once sampled some of the plants. She was just nibbling a broccoli leaf when she was startled by vibrations made by approaching footsteps.

A young girl came into the garden to pick vegetables for the family table. Daisy ran quickly and silently to find the escape hole, but in her panic she could not locate it. She bumped into the wire repeatedly, then backtracked and hid among the broccoli leaves. But the young girl had spotted her and quickly caught her.

14

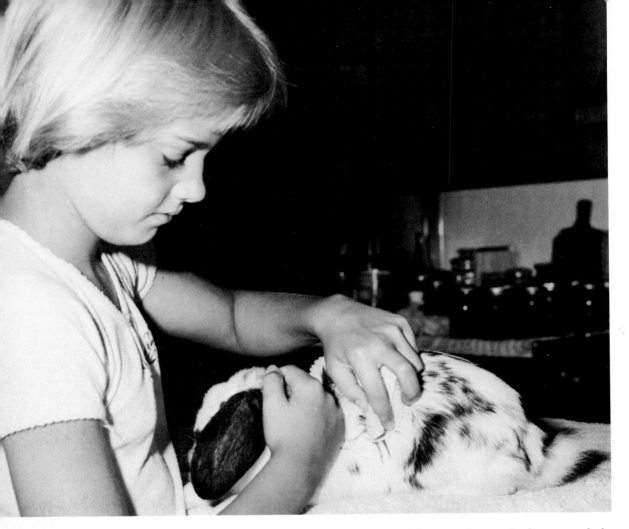

The girl stroked the trembling rabbit gently and then took it home. When she looked at Daisy more closely she noticed some dried blood and the hanging ears. The girl thought they must be broken. After she had washed the dried blood away she tried to make the ears stand up, but they always dropped down again. The girl remembered her dog, Honey. When Honey had been just a puppy, her ears were hanging down, and a veterinarian had taped them in an erect position. After several months he had removed the tape and the ears stood up straight and firm.

With the help of two Popsicle sticks and some gauze and adhesive tape, the girl taped Daisy's ears so that they stood erect. It was not a very good job, because the little rabbit struggled and kicked, trying to get away. Daisy jumped about wildly, shook her head, and then with her front paws she quickly tore the annoying bandages and tape away. But even then Daisy did not calm down. She hid under the bed, ran into the kitchen wall, and dirtied the living-room carpet. Finally the girl put Daisy into a cardboard box that had holes for ventilation cut into it. She placed a few lettuce leaves into the box, but no water, and then tied up the box securely for the rest of the day and the entire night.

June 24 When the girl opened the box in the morning, Daisy was a sorry sight. She was weak, dirty, and listless, and the box was chewed up, wet, and foul-smelling. The lettuce leaves were untouched. The girl's mother suggested taking the rabbit to a veterinarian right away.

When the vet heard the girl's worries about the ears, he laughed and explained that this breed of rabbit was supposed to have hanging ears. He said the breed was called Mini Lops, a

variety of several lop-eared breeds. Lop-eared rabbits are some of the oldest breeds known. Mini Lops are believed (but it is not certain) to have appeared first in Algeria, North Africa, and later they were imported to France, Belgium, the Netherlands, and England. In England, through selective breeding, the ears became longer and longer and the offspring of those rabbits were called English Lops. The ears of the French Lops are much shorter. Miniature versions of the French Lops, rabbits like Daisy, have become very popular pets recently. They come in many colors and color patterns. They weigh about five to eight pounds at maturity. Mini Lops have a nice temperament and are mostly raised for pets or shows.

The vet continued to explain that the commercial rabbit pellets were the best way to feed a pet rabbit, whatever its breed, since this kind of food is nutritionally balanced. About six ounces or one cup per day is all a rabbit needs to eat. A little hay and a few leafy greens would be a welcome treat. Fresh water, a very essential part in the proper care of rabbits, must be available at all times. A rabbit also needs an airy cage to live in, and the cage must be kept very clean. Almost casually, the vet mentioned that this rabbit probably had escaped from the rabbit farm several miles away, where the breeder had just started to raise Mini Lops.

The young girl was startled. She had never given any thought to where her fancy rabbit might have come from. The idea that she might have to give it up was almost too much to bear. She worried all day about what she should do. Her parents suggested that she call the breeder, tell him how she had found the rabbit, and ask if she could buy it.

June 25   It took the girl till the following morning to make the call. She need not have worried. The breeder was very nice. He suggested that she keep the rabbit, take good care of it, bring it in for breeding when it was older, and share the resulting litter of young with him. He also invited the girl to come over on July 19 to attend a 4-H Club meeting, led by his wife. The members of this group of boys and girls were interested in raising, breeding, and exhibiting domestic rabbits of all kinds.

June 28   Since the little rabbit was going to become a permanent member of the family, the girl gave her the name Daisy, while her father started to build a rabbit hutch from a sketch the rabbit breeder had sent over. After four nights in a makeshift crate, Daisy was put into her new home. The rabbit jumped about excitedly, twitching her whiskers, and sniffing out every nook and corner. Daisy's cage at the rabbit farm had been a commercial, sanitary, all-wire cage. The new homemade cage had a wooden frame 4 feet by 3 feet and was 2½ feet high. It was mounted against the wall of the garage. The sides of the cage had 1 inch by 2 inch wire, but the wire on the bottom of the

cage was a special kind, ½ inch by 1 inch, so that the rabbit's feet could not get caught in it, but with openings large enough so that the droppings could fall through. One end of the hutch had a roomy wooden sleeping compartment lined with straw, which would have to be scrubbed with soap and water once a week to keep it clean. (If rabbits are kept on a dirty floor, they might get sore or infected feet and hocks, and other diseases.) A solid roof sheltered the cage from the elements.

Daisy immediately investigated the water supply. The water bottle hung on the outside of the cage with the drinking tube reaching inside the pen. That way Daisy always could sip water that was fresh and clean. For the first few days the old water dish was still left inside the pen, just in case Daisy did not know how to drink out of the tube. Her pellets were served in a special metal feeder securely hung on the wire inside the cage. (Some people fasten the feeder on the outside, with the hopper protruding to the inside through an opening cut into the wire.)

June 29   Every day Daisy was taken to the house for play, grooming, and petting by her young mistress. After her first shyness, Daisy seemed to enjoy hopping about the house and investigating everything. She jumped on chairs, then down quickly to hide in the kitchen near the garbage pail. She learned that the refrigerator might hold some greens or a carrot and as soon as the door was opened Daisy came hopping over. She was never disappointed. She learned to use a cat litter box and never soiled the house.

July 19 The day of the 4-H Club meeting at the rabbit farm was hot and sunny. Daisy rode in a cage in back of the car and was then carried to the meeting site, a small clearing in the wood adjoining the breeder's house. A makeshift table had been set up and a dozen boys and girls were standing or sitting around. Most of them had rabbits by their sides.

The rabbit breeder's wife started the meeting by introducing a few new members. She advised everyone to put their rabbits in a shady place, since rabbits can easily get heat stroke.

Addressing herself to the new members, she said that some of the boys and girls would tell their fellow club members about their own particular breed of rabbit so that everyone could learn about the various domestic breeds. She explained that there are more than fifty different breeds of rabbits known, but that only six or seven kinds of the popular breeds were represented in this club.

She then put a large white rabbit on the table and told her audience that this was a New Zealand White, the kind raised on her farm, with the exception of a few fancy rabbits. She owned about 200 New Zealand White rabbits, and they were all raised outdoors in wire cages. Those rabbits made good pets, but were usually raised for meat, laboratory use, and to show. Rabbit meat, which is very nutritious, has become quite popular. The meat is white and firm. It can be found in some supermarkets in the frozen-meat section. More than 500,000 rabbits are used in laboratories every year, but a license is required to fulfill the special laboratory needs.

She told the children that New Zealand rabbits come in red, white, and black colors. They are a large breed and can weigh

up to twelve pounds. They are gentle and very hardy. They were probably one of the first American-bred rabbits that supposedly were developed from a cross between a white rabbit and a Belgian hare (a domestic rabbit from Belgium). They did not come from New Zealand. They first became known in California and Indiana about 1922.

The New Zealand White is an albino animal. Its fur is always white and its eyes are red. A black phase of the New Zealand rabbit has just become popular in recent years.

After the 4-H leader had finished and everyone had petted the rabbit, a girl with a very well-known breed of rabbit was the next speaker. Her rabbit was a Dutch, the kind most often sold in stores at Easter time, and the breed usually portrayed in picture books about rabbits. It originated in Holland and was introduced into England around 1864. The Dutch rabbit almost

immediately became a favorite pet and show animal, and was soon bred in many countries. It is a small breed, weighing from four to five pounds when fully grown. It is easy to care for and very gentle. The fur pattern is genetically controlled, which means that the basic pattern is always the same, although its color can vary. The Dutch is a colored rabbit with white markings, and not a white rabbit with colored markings. The colors can be black, blue, gray, tortoise, chocolate, or tan. The pattern is clean and sharply defined. The white forms the saddle and the blaze and covers all of the front feet but only about 1½ inches of the hind feet.

The next rabbit that was put on the table by its owner was called a Netherland Dwarf. It is probably the smallest breed of domestic rabbits. It weighs only 2 to 2½ pounds and is very friendly and gentle. It has dense fur that comes in a multitude of

colors, including lilac, sable, opal, black, white, and brown. The Netherland Dwarf is believed to have originated in Holland, the result of breeding a Polish rabbit (another very small domestic breed) with a small native wild rabbit. It was accepted as a breed by the American Rabbit Breeders Association in the U.S.A. in 1969.

Daisy's owner was now asked to talk about her unusual rabbit. She put Daisy on the table and told the members all that she had just recently learned about the breed of Mini Lops.

29

The next rabbit shown was truly amazing. Its ears were huge and hung long and low. It was an English Lop. This rabbit usually sits with its head held low, which shows off the ears to good advantage. (The longest ears on record measured 28½

inches.) It makes a very good pet because it has a loving disposition. This breed comes in many colors, solid, or in color combinations (called broken) and can weigh up to eleven pounds at maturity.

When an Angora rabbit was put up next on the table, all the members let out cries of "Oh, how cute," and "Look how beautiful," or "What is that?" An Angora rabbit looks very different from other rabbits because of its long, fluffy wool.

(Angora fur is called wool.) The French and the English Angora rabbit look very similar, but the wool of the English Angora is more silky. It is not a very large rabbit, weighing from six to eight pounds when fully grown. It probably originated in Turkey and its wool was and still is high-priced. In France the breed was improved and a market was created for the fine wool. The first Angora rabbits probably had the color of a wild rabbit, and the white color was achieved later through selective breeding. There are also black, blue, and fawn-colored Angoras. The Angora rabbit needs a lot of care. The wool is so finely textured that it tends to mat and knot. It must be groomed every few days to prevent this. Matting is not only unsightly, but it destroys the value of the wool and is painful and disturbing to the animal.

The wool can be clipped, sheared, or plucked. The simplest method for the beginner is to use sharp scissors, or a comb. Every time the rabbit is combed, loose wool will come out. The

wool should be saved, and soon there will be enough to make a scarf or mittens. Angora wool is often used in combination with other fibers for men's and women's clothing. The presence of the Angora makes all materials warmer, lighter, and softer.

The last club member to speak had a large rabbit called a Red Satin. He told his fellow 4-Hers that a Satin is easily recognized by its short, velvety, dense fur that has a special satiny gloss or sheen. This rabbit is a mutation (a change from the standard). It was first noticed in the mid-thirties in a litter of rabbits of a breed called Havana. The farmer who had bred them experimented with rebreeding them when they were mature, and found that they formed a truly separate group. But it took a while until this breed was recognized by the Rabbit Breeders Association and was permitted to compete in shows. Satins are now bred in nine different colors. It is a very friendly rabbit and can weigh twelve pounds when mature.

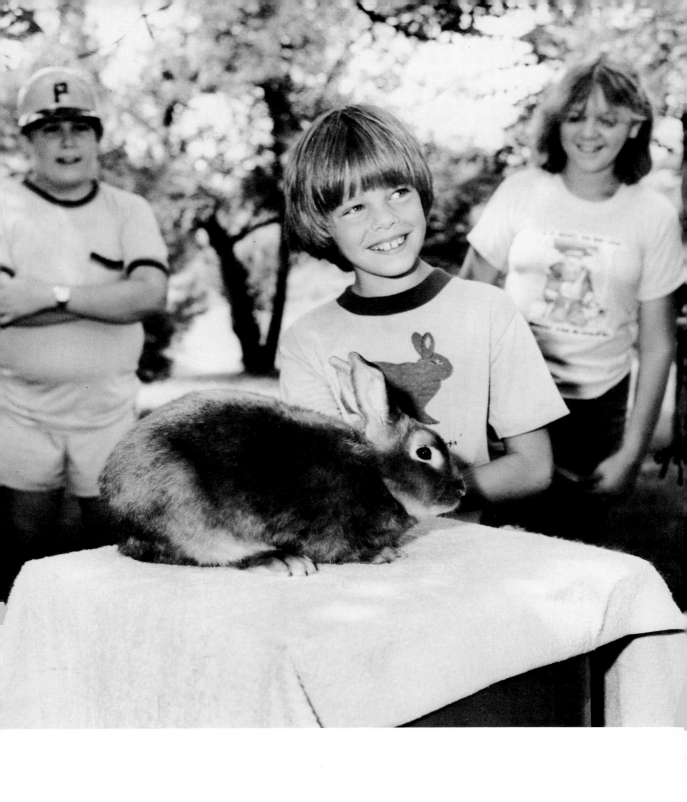

The meeting closed with a round of applause for the speakers, and a slice of carrot for each of the rabbits. The members were reminded that the next month's meeting would be the last before the big rabbit show at the county fair. All rabbits to be entered should be brought to that meeting so that they could be weighed and tattooed for the show.

Daisy's owner had learned a lot about rabbits and she had made many new friends. She wanted to enter Daisy in the forthcoming show, and the breeder gave her helpful hints as to good health and grooming to get her rabbit into top show condition.

July 28 Daisy led a good life. She grew quickly and at three months was almost adult size. Her coat was sleek and her eyes bright. Her owner gave her high-quality pellets, some extra vitamins and minerals, and saw to it that Daisy's teeth were kept in good condition. Rabbits' long front teeth (incisors) must be filed down. Otherwise, they would keep on growing and growing until they would get so long that the rabbit could not chew any more and would starve to death. When a rabbit chews on hard things, its teeth are filed automatically. The pellets Daisy ate were hard, but that was not enough. The young girl provided Daisy with small blocks of wood and sometimes fruitwood twigs on which to chew.

Because of a rabbit's large incisors, many people think that they are rodents. They are not. Rodents have one pair of incisors, rabbits have two pairs. One can see the second pair right behind the front pair. For that reason scientists have put rabbits into an order of their own called *lagomorpha*.

Daisy got used to being handled, but she never liked to be picked up, and would kick and struggle if someone tried. Since the young girl had seen how the rabbit breeder's wife had handled her rabbits she tried to do the same. She tucked Daisy under one arm and supported the animal's rump with her other arm and hand. That way, Daisy felt more secure and relaxed when she was being carried around. Picking up a rabbit by its ears should not be attempted, since it hurts the rabbit and might injure the ears.

August 16 At the next 4-H meeting, boys and girls were helped by the leader to fill out their entry blanks for the rabbit show. The rabbits that were to be entered had to be purebred. That meant that their parents, grandparents, and even their great-grandparents had to all be of the same breed. Each rabbit had to have an identification number tattooed on the inside of its ear to be eligible for competition. The rabbit farmer did this for the members. After the tattooing, the rabbits were weighed. A rabbit that was over or under weight did not have much chance of winning. Each breed of rabbit had to conform to a standard set for that breed by the American Rabbit Breeders Association. The standard was a blueprint, or model, of what a breed should look like. Such perfection is seldom achieved, but breeders try to come as close as possible to it, and the judge in a show selects the one rabbit that comes closest to that standard as a winner.

August 28   The day before the show, long lines of cars, trucks, and trailers arrived at the fairgrounds to set up the exhibits. Women and girls brought their needlework and embroidery, their paintings, flowers, jams, or pies to display. Farmers, young and old, brought samples of the largest ears of corn, the biggest pumpkins, the sweetest grapes, or the most fragrant hay. In the buildings reserved for livestock exhibits, one could hear horses stamping their feet, and whinnying nervously. Cows, calves, and bulls were driven into their stalls with much shouting by their handlers, and loud, protesting noises from the animals. Lambs and sheep were bleating, pigs squealing and grunting, and chickens, ducks, geese, and pigeons each vocalized in their own special way. Only the rabbits and guinea pigs were silent.

The rabbits and the cavies (guinea pigs) were housed and shown together in a separate building. The exhibitors had brought their animals in small carrying cages, and then had placed them in one of the rows and rows of numbered cages provided by the show officials. They fed and watered their charges and then left them. A few volunteers stay the night to safeguard the animals and see to their needs. Daisy, who had been fed and watered, and given a few greens as an extra treat by her owner, was very nervous and restless, and it took her a long time to settle down and doze off.

August 29   Early this morning the judges arrived and went to work immediately. Each rabbit was brought to the judges' table by a special handler. The judges weighed the animal, checked its fur, teeth, bone structure, and general appearance.

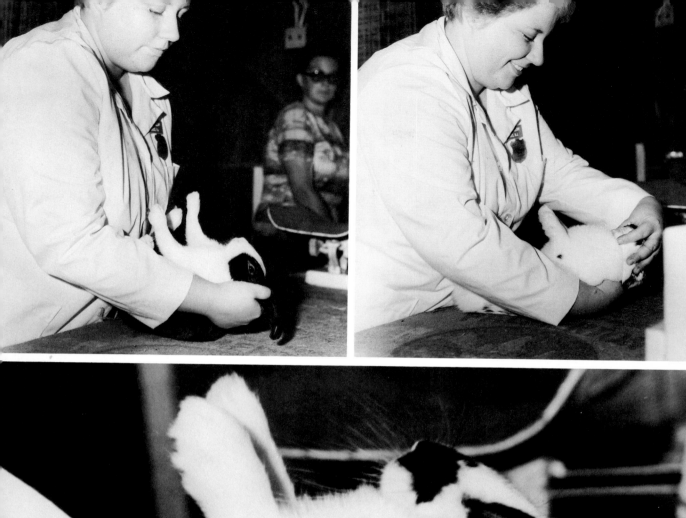

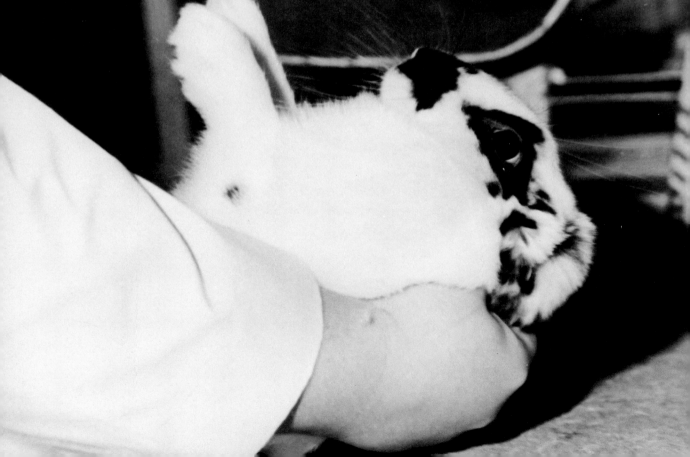

Then the rabbits were put into a holding pen until all the rabbits in the group had been seen. Each breed was divided by variety, sex, and age, and each group was judged separately. By comparing all the rabbits in a given group, the judges could eliminate the poorer specimens and award the prize to the best in that group. From the group winners the judges selected the best of each breed. At the end of the judging the breed winners were brought out again and judged against each other so that the best rabbit in the show could be selected. Daisy won best of her group, which was for female rabbits under six months of age. The best of show was won by another 4-H member for her New Zealand White. Daisy's owner was very proud and excited when she stepped forward to get her trophy, and Daisy was rewarded with a slice of carrot when she got home.

September 5 Shortly after the show, Daisy's disposition changed. She was very restless and bounced and jumped around her cage. She was not as friendly as she had been and resisted petting or being picked up. The young girl became worried and called the rabbit breeder for advice. The breeder thought that Daisy should be bred. He said that the smell of the other rabbits at the show might have given Daisy the idea that she wanted a mate. Although Daisy was just a little over five months old, the breeder thought it was a good time to breed her.

September 10 On this bright day in September, Daisy was taken to the rabbit farm and put into the hutch of a prize-winning buck. He was of the agouti color, just like Daisy's mother had been. There was no doubt that the two rabbits were willing to breed. A quick sniff to get acquainted, a hop and a jump around the pen, and before one could see what was happening, the mating was over. The young girl could not believe it, and asked if the mating had really taken place. The breeder explained that they would take Daisy out of the pen now, but repeat the breeding in half an hour just to make sure.

The second mating was over just as quickly as the first one had been, but the girl had noticed the strange behavior of the male. Almost immediately after mounting the female the buck fell off on his side for just an instant, then hopped away and groomed himself. That meant the mating had indeed taken place.

September 11 Back home Daisy became her friendly self again. It takes four to five weeks after mating for the doe to

44

kindle (give birth). During this time she must receive plenty of good food and be kept in top physical condition.

September 29   By the end of the month Daisy grew restless, and the girl put a narrow wooden nesting box into the cage. Daisy inspected the straw-filled box and after a few minutes she started to pull out soft fur from her chest and abdomen to line the nest. It was as if she had done it before, or as if someone had shown her what to do. During the next few days she spent a lot of time rearranging her nesting material and adding more soft fur to it. She looked a bit plumper and was less active. She did not enjoy playing at her owner's house anymore and seemed to be lost in a world of her own.

October 9   When the girl came to feed Daisy on this crisp autumn morning Daisy was sitting on top of the nestbox. By her contented expression the girl knew that her pet had given birth during the night. She peeked into the nestbox and five tiny bunnies lay inside, sleeping soundly. Two were black and white like Daisy, one was all black, the fourth one blue-gray, and the fifth one was agouti color like the father. The perpetuation of the race had gone full circle. Daisy, at the age of six months, was a devoted mother, knowing by instinct how to care for and how to protect her babies, until they could look after themselves.

Index